DEDICATION

This book is dedicated to the owner who feels like life isn't complete without multiple dogs. May this book bring you the knowledge and skill to keep your multi-dog household peaceful, loving and full of memory making antics.

Multiple Dog Household: A guide to training and problem-solving

Nikki Ivey

ISBN:1495452700
ISBN-13:9781495452703

CONTENTS

ACKNOWLEDGMENTS

I want to thank Britteny Watson for the amazing job she does with editing and formatting my work. You truly understand how to make my words on paper be as good as the words that come from my mouth. I also want to thank her for all of her support and love. To my clients, thank you for allowing me into your life. Most importantly, I want to thank God for the gift that He has given me; may I carry it always.

Introduction

Recent research shows that 73% of Americans own dogs. Of those, 28% own two dogs, while 12% own three or more. There are many reasons people have multi-dog homes. Some decide to forgo having children and have pets instead. Others feel their first dog should have a companion. And some acquire multiple dogs when they show up in their yards one day. Whatever the reason, the number of multi-dog homes is definitely on the rise.

Having multiple dogs in one household has many benefits, but there are also many problems that could arise if owners do not take the time to educate themselves on how to handle the obstacles they may face by having more than one dog. Whether you want to add another dog to your home or you already have multiple dogs, I want to give you a resource to establish a successful, smooth-running household.

I will explain the pros and cons of having a multi-dog household. I'll also discuss the best way to choose a new housemate, and how to prevent and solve common pack issues.

I recommend that everyone in your household read this book as it essential for everyone in a family to be on the same page. A divided house of humans will result in a divided house of canines.

Chapter I:

Choosing to be a Multi-Dog Household

There are many benefits to having more than one dog, especially if there are multiple humans in the home. Having multiple dogs allows each human to have a "buddy," and teaches children to share in the responsibilities associated with taking care of "their" dog. Multiple dogs can also keep one another company on rainy or long days, or when you are too tired to provide physical activity for your dog. As you know, I constantly advocate dog-dog socialization. Though it is important for dogs to socialize with dogs from other packs, having multiple dogs helps build a foundation on which your dogs' communication skills can grow. It is important if you have multiple dogs in your home, however, that you do not rely on an older or more established dog to train the younger or new dog. Though dogs can learn behaviors from other dogs, it is solely your responsibility to ensure your dogs are receiving proper training, and learn appropriate behaviors.

There are also some cons to owning more than one dog. If you are the only human occupant of your home, you may find that having multiple dogs is overwhelming, and may put a strain on your finances and time. Before adopting or integrating a new dog into your home, think about whether or not you can afford to do so. If you are not the only occupant in the home, and especially if you have children, you must again look at the time and money that must be invested into having multiple dogs. I often have clients who have difficulty managing more than one dog, especially if one or both have behavioral, health or manner issues. The most common issues I see are clients not being able to walk, train or socialize two dogs simultaneously.

When considering if you should bring another dog into your home, first ask yourself the following questions:

1. Do I have the finances to handle more than one dog? What if one dog gets sick, can I afford healthcare?
2. Do I have time to give more than one dog my attention? Do I have time to separate them so they each get one-on-one time with me?
3. Do I have my established dog trained? Does he know all the crucial real life manners?
4. Do I have time to train my new dog to the standards of real life manners?
5. Will I be able to handle them both out in public for trips to the dog park? Family gatherings? Vacations?
6. Can I afford to hire a professional if the two dogs develop problems toward one another?

7. Am I willing to part with the new dog if it doesn't integrate well into my established pack?
8. If I meet a partner who also has a dog, will three or more dogs be too much to handle?

If you answer these questions, and find that adding a new dog is a feasible option for your household, then it is time to choose the correct dog for your lifestyle. Below are some steps and guidelines for picking the right dog.

First, look at your reason for wanting a second (or third and so on) dog. Do you want a companion for your existing dog or dogs? A dog for your second child? Look at who or what the dog's purpose will be.

Keep in mind that the sex of dog you get does not necessarily matter. Many believe that in order to keep peace among a pack they must automatically choose a new dog of the opposite sex. Only you know if your current dog has an issue with dogs of the same or opposite sex, and this should be taken into consideration before bringing a new dog into your home. I have seen problems arise within a pack regardless of the sexes of the dogs. If your dog is not historically a fan of dogs of the same sex, but you are adamant in wanting the same sex, then look deeper into the issue. The issue may arise from size or personality differences, and not necessarily the fact that your female dog dislikes all other females.

You should also consider your dog's personality before getting a new dog. Is your dog laid back or playful and outgoing? You may want to get a dog with the opposite personality as this can teach your current dog to problem solve in order to prevent conflict, and develop his own communication skills. Try some play dates with friends' dogs to see how your dog reacts to different personalities.

Keep you living arrangements in mind when choosing a new dog. Do you rent a property that only allows small dogs or certain breeds? Do you have enough room in your home to accommodate the space needs of a large dog?

Age can play a part to how two dogs bond. An older dog can benefit from having a younger dog in the home as a younger dog is more likely to keep the older dog active, thus increasing his life span. An older dog can also help with correcting and teaching dog language skills to a younger dog. If you get two dogs too close together in age, you may run into issues such as dealing with end of life care at the same time. If you get two puppies at the same time, keep in mind you will have double the work with issues such as housebreaking and chewing. In order for dogs to learn proper communication skills, they need interaction with dogs that are at different maturity levels. I typically recommend at least a year in age between dogs.

I typically do not recommend getting littermates that have been together since birth. Many feel that having littermates will allow the dogs to have a lifelong partner and that they will provide one another dog interaction and/or help develop the communication skills all puppies and dogs require. In my experience, littermates rarely live together harmoniously. This is because oftentimes we as humans do not assist in the development of the dogs' individual personalities and communication skills as we expect them to do this for one another. When we do not provide leadership, conflict arises, and many times at least one dog has behavioral issues related to the lack of socialization and human intervention. Even when humans do provide proper intervention and training, the two dogs must be allowed to develop their own personalities. Again, dogs require interaction from dogs with differing maturity levels and skills.

If you do have littermates, provide individual training for each dog. Separation from their sibling is important as this will allow each dog to develop its own skills and personality. This is also true of dogs that are not littermates but are close in age.

CHAPTER II
BASICS OF TRAINING

Part I
Developing Good Habits

Before you bring a new dog home, or before you attempt to train multiple dogs at once, you must develop good habits as the leader of your home. When most people train their dog they focus on the basics of sit, stay, down, come and heel. These behaviors are beneficial, but they do not necessarily set the dog up for success in the real world. Because a dog will sit on command in a kitchen at dinnertime does not mean he will have self-control and sit when guests arrive, let alone if they bring a strange dog. This is why it is imperative that you build a foundation that allows the dog to extrapolate proper behaviors in all areas of his life. This foundation is especially important if you have more than one dog in your household.

Secrets to the REWARD

Dog trainers and behavioral consultants often debate what the proper reward for a dog is that offers a desired behavior. Traditional trainers scoff at the thought of using food or treats, because they consider it bribery. However, they often misunderstand the proper way to use it. Any reward can be used as bribery or as a lure. The real answer is; it does not matter what you use for a reward as long as your dog finds it desirable. Your job is to reward properly.

I teach three ways to acknowledge good behavior: 1. A verbal mark, such as "good boy/girl." 2. A verbal mark with petting. 3. A verbal mark with a resource, such as food or a toy.

Rewarding properly will help your dog understand what behaviors you want to see repeated. When you get into the habit of telling him "yes" or "good" for proper behavior, he will focus and repeat that behavior in hopes of receiving your attention (a reward). Think of yourself as a slot machine--pay out intermittently, but pay out big. For instance, your dog performs a proper behavior ten times. Of those ten behaviors, you reward him four times with food, three times with a pet, and three times with a positive verbal mark. This is variable reinforcement, or what I like to call, "the slot machine system." The dog anticipates a reward, but does not know which reward will be divvied out. This heightens his desire to do as he is instructed.

Never have food in your hand when waiting for your dog to offer a behavior. You may have it on a counter, in a bowl or put away in a cabinet, but focus on marking the good behavior first with praise or a clicker before worrying about what type of food reward you are going to give.

All dogs are motivated by food. If your dog is not eating his regular food, it does not mean he is not food motivated, it means he either does not like the taste of his food or it is causing him discomfort. I recommend trying a variety of healthy, and nutritional foods to see what works best. A food reward should be a treat small enough to be consumed quickly and yet large enough to taste. "Jackpot" rewards (consisting of a handful of small treats and dispensed with an overabundance of enthusiasm) can be used, but sparingly. A jackpot will leave a big impression on the dog and will raise the likelihood that the behavior will be repeated.

I recommend putting together a mix of different treats I call a "doggie Chex Mix." These treats should vary in flavors and textures.

Secrets to using CONSEQUENCES

Training consists of positive and negative responses. People typically associate positive with "good" and negative with "bad." Think of positive and negative in mathematical terms instead. Positive means "to add" and negative means "to take away." Giving a positive response or consequence means you give the dog something it wants, (i.e. attention or a treat.) Negative responses or consequences occur when you take something away. For instance, by ignoring you are taking attention away. People often think negative consequences only consist of harsh punishment such as the use of a correction collar, a knee in the chest or a zap from an electronic collar. These are negative in a traditional sense ("bad"), and typically do not facilitate the learning process. By using harsh methods, you are only teaching the dog to avoid pain by suppressing certain behaviors. Often dogs will shut down or stop trying to problem solve because of fear when these harsh techniques are used. These definitions will make it easier to understand the difference in positive and negative consequences:

Positive Reinforcement:

When using this technique you are adding something good to the dog to get a behavior repeated. For example, when your dog sits and you give him a treat or praise.

Negative Reinforcement:

When using negative reinforcement you are taking away something unpleasant in order to get the dog to repeat a behavior. For instance, shocking a dog with an e-collar until it comes, or chocking a dog with a collar until he sits. I never recommend these methods because they are dangerous and out of date.

Positive Punishment:

Positive punishment occurs when you add something unpleasant to extinguish a behavior. When some trainers use leash pops to extinguish pulling on leash or a zap by an e-collar to extinguish barking, they are using positive punishment. I do not recommend this type of punishment because, like negative reinforcement, it can also extinguish a dog's desire to try new behaviors because it causes fear. I also do not use positive punishment because in order for it to be successful a person must know how to use proper timing and how not to harm a dog physically.

Negative Punishment:

By taking away something good from the dog in order to extinguish a behavior you are using negative punishment. You can show a dog that is jumping on you that the behavior is not acceptable by utilizing a body turn and ignoring. By doing this you are taking away something good—attention.

When training, you should use positive reinforcement and negative punishment only. This will allow you to be less than perfect with your timing and still receive results. Always remain calm, confident and consistent when giving consequences.

There are a number of consequences you can use when you see a behavior from your dog that you wish to extinguish. Keep in mind that not every dog is going to see something as a consequence, so you have to do a little problem-solving yourself to determine the best one to use. For instance, taking attention away from a dog that does not seem to crave attention will not help extinguish a behavior, however, taking away a treat may. Here are some consequences you can use to extinguish an undesirable behavior:

- Taking attention away from the dog
- Putting dog in time-out
- Not putting on leash
- Not taking off leash
- Not throwing toy
- Not feeding immediately
- Not allowing out of crate immediately
- Stopping play

As I mentioned above, ignoring (not looking or touching the dog) is a technique used to extinguish behavior that is not self-rewarding, (a behavior such as chewing is self-rewarding) but you must do it correctly.

Self-rewarding behavior is a behavior the dog does that rewards without you being involved. When dealing with self-rewarding behaviors, such as chewing or barking, you cannot simply ignore the dog. You must interrupt these behaviors instead of ignoring them. Even when you interrupt you do not have to do it harshly. Interrupt with the least amount of interaction so that the dog does not interpret your acknowledgement as a reward.

Another common self-rewarding behavior is counter surfing when food is present. If there is nothing on the counter within the dog's reach, the behavior is not self-rewarding. There is nothing to gain. If this is the case, ignore the behavior. The dog will learn that nothing is on the counter and will eventually stop trying. For those times when the dog is successful at getting food off of the counter, you can either push the item farther back or you can implement a split-up between the dog and the counter, interrupting his attempt. You do not want to talk to the dog during this exercise because you need to interrupt with the least amount of interaction. You want the dog to learn that counter surfing never works, not that it works unless someone is there to interrupt.

If your dog is chewing on the rug, give a calm "nope," gently remove the dog from the object being chewed on, and give him something else to chew on. Expect the dog to go back to the rug as he tries to figure out why you interrupted him. When he does, simply interrupt again. When the dog does it three times in a row implement a time-out.

Puppies often chew in order to soothe the pain of teething. I recommend having a variety of toys on hand. For older dogs, supply deer antlers or hard bones (but not rawhide).

Implementing a TIME-OUT

A time-out occurs when a dog is isolated from an event for a certain amount of time due to an inappropriate behavior. Time-outs can be used anywhere for anything. There are rules that you must follow, in order to make it successful.

I use a "three strikes and you are out" rule. Once I give a dog three chances to do the correct behavior by ignoring or interrupting, I implement a time-out. Most time-outs are done for self-rewarding behaviors.

When giving a time-out, be sure you do not show emotion. A true leader does not show emotion when giving a negative consequence. Remain calm and matter-of-fact. Use either a leash, the collar, or if the dog is small enough, carry him to his time-out space; be sure you do not pet or talk to him in the process. If you use the collar, grab the side and use the slightest pressure possible. Do not grab the dog by the scruff.

Time-out areas can change depending on your circumstances. When at home, use a crate or small room as the isolation space. The dog will not see the crate or room as a negative unless you display anger or frustration. If you are out in public you can use your car, a portable crate or just take the dog away from the action and have him stand beside you on leash. If you are at the dog park and the dog misbehaves three times, put him on leash and take him outside the dog park.

When giving time-outs, start with thirty-second intervals and increase as needed. When a time-out is completed, ensure the dog earns his freedom by exhibiting self-control, and that he receives a permission word such as "okay." Do not be surprised if your dog attempts the inappropriate behavior again; he is only trying to figure out what caused the time-out. Once you have given your dog several opportunities with the "three strikes rule" and the dog begins to understand what behaviors are inappropriate, commence with decreasing to two strikes, then one strike and eventually immediate time-out. Most dogs do not get to the immediate time-out when the technique is used properly.

A time-out is appropriate when you are teaching your dog to stop jumping on the furniture. When the dog jumps on the furniture, remove him without speaking. Once he is on the floor, go back about your business. If he continues to jump on the furniture, remove him two more times. When he gets on the furniture a fourth time, take him to his crate or to an isolated room. Leave him for thirty seconds. If he is calm, release him with a permission word, and repeat if necessary. Allow three strikes for the first few days, and then decrease the chances until he begins to understand what you want.

If you are out in public you may have to be more creative. Let's say you ask the dog to sit. If your dog understands the command and refuses, give him three chances and then implement a time-out. If your car is close by, put him in it. If you have a crate, use that. Whatever you do, be sure you do not allow anything good to take place until he sits on his own without you forcing him. Once he is released, take him back to the exact place you asked for the sit and ask for it again. Repeat the process

Mark *during* the desired behavior, and not after it is completed or as the dog moves onto another behavior. For example, if you like for your dog to sit, wait for him to begin to sit. As the dog's bottom is moving towards the floor, mark it with "yes" and give him a piece of food. Reward all positive behavior. ANY behavior that you do not mind seeing again, no matter how small, need to be marked. Good manners can be walking by the cat without chasing it, or not barking at a noise outside. These are behaviors that you want to see repeated, so mark and feed.

Lastly, the dog must do something physically different to earn a mark and a piece of food. He is not allowed to just sit and stare at you. This means he is not problem solving, but simply waiting to be fed. If your dog does not want to work for the food, he does not eat. If this happens several times than you need to change his food.

Let's break this exercise down into steps:

1. Grab your dog's food bowl and fill it up with his normal amount of food for that feeding.
2. Sit somewhere comfortable, where your dog is going to have plenty of room to work. You do not have to sit on the floor.
3. Place the bowl in your lap and use your hands to cover the bowl, *if* the dog is trying to put his nose in it. Do not move the bowl out of the dog's reach or tell the dog to leave

it. He is offering an inappropriate behavior, so, simply cover the bowl and ignore him.

4. Stay silent throughout the process until your dog gives you a behavior that you would like to see repeated. When he offers a behavior that you want, mark it with your marker and give a piece of food.

5. Wait for him to offer something different and repeat.

6. If he gives you a behavior that you do not like followed by a good behavior, be sure the good behavior is exhibited for at least three seconds before recognizing. The pause only happens if the good is following a bad behavior.

This process may take between 15-45 minutes, depending on the dog's confidence level and problem-solving skills. When beginning this technique feed the entire bowl this way. Do not feed half the bowl by hand and then place the bowl down for the remainder of the feeding. If your dog does not earn all of his food in the time allotted, put the food away and try again later. It is not unusual for a dog to leave a portion of his food when first beginning this technique. I recommend feeding this way, at least once a day, unless you have a very nervous or shy dog, then hand feed both feedings.

Regular Feeding:

Just because you allow a dog to eat all of his

or come in without permission. This not only demeans your leadership status, it is dangerous.

If you have to hold your dog's collar or give him a command so that he does not bound out the door, then you are not allowing your dog to problem-solve and think for himself. Dogs should learn that going out a door is not an option, unless he is given permission to do so. You should control any threshold that the dog has to cross.

The first step is to establish a permission word. Again, I use "okay." Food will not be used during this exercise since the reward is the ability to move over a threshold.

Start this exercise on leash so that you can limit your dog's ability to move away from the door. Do not use the leash to control where the dog is standing, or to pull the dog away or through the door. Use a leash that limits the dog's movement to only a foot or two ahead of you. Slip your hand into the handle and tuck your thumb into your pocket. Keep the leash loose so that it looks like a 'J' hanging next to his collar. Do not ask your dog to sit for this exercise; in "real life," your dog will be confronted with many open door opportunities, and in those situations, he will more than likely be standing.

Next, start to open the door. Expect your dog to move forward. The moment he moves forward, close the door. Be quick, but try not to slam his head in the door. When the door begins to close he should back up; if he does not, do not pull him back with the leash. Give him a few seconds to back up by gently pushing the door into him. If that does not make him back up, remove your hand from the door and take a step or two backwards with your thumb still hooked in your pocket. This will make him back up with you. Once he is back inside, close the door. Immediately begin opening the door again. Each time he moves forward close the door until he backs up. You may or may not get the door all the way closed before he starts backing up. The moment he backs up, begin opening it again. Be sure your timing is correct. Open the door when the dog is away from it, and close it if he moves forward. Once the dog is stationary, and you have the door open enough for the dog to go through, give him permission to pass over the threshold and out the door. His reward will be to sniff around outside for a minute. When you come back in, do the same exercise. Each time you practice, try to get the door open a little farther before permission is given and increase the time your dog has to wait. There may be times when you want him to go out immediately without waiting. This is fine, just be sure you give permission before he starts to move through the door. You do not have to be the first one through the door. Allowing the dog to exit first will not undermine your leadership role.

With a crate or car door your dog will not be on leash, so your timing will have to be faster. If the dog gets through a door without permission, you must physically bring him back to repeat the exercise. Do this calmly and with confidence.

It does not take a dog long to understand the goal of this exercise. After the first two to three times your dog has to show restraint, gradually increase the difficulty (i.e. the length of time that your dog must wait before passing through the threshold.) Remember, each time you increase the difficulty, your dog may take a step back in his training. This is normal. Stay consistent, do not verbalize your frustration, and wait for the dog to make the decision to not go through the door until he is given permission.

With multiple dogs, start with one dog at a time to help them understand what you want. When they are beginning to understand it individually, you can start putting two dogs together. When allowing two dogs at the door you may allow them to go out together by giving the permission word or you may give them individual permission by saying their name first before giving the permission word. If the dogs run out the door before given permission, simply bring them back in and start again. For example, Dayin and Jake are at the back door waiting to come in. I need to wipe each dog's paws before allowing them in. Due to the layout of the house, I can only do this with one dog at a time. So I open the door, say "Dayin, okay" and allow her inside. If Jake follows without permission, I get him gently by the collar and put him back outside. I wipe Dayin's paws and give her permission to walk away. I then follow up with Jake by opening the door and giving him permission.

By expecting each dog to have control you can

prevent a lot of issues at the door. Small dogs will not get trampled by large dogs and fights will not occur because you are teaching self-control as well as taking on the leadership role.

Allowing Pets on Furniture:

I enjoy asking my clients if they freely allow their dogs on the furniture; their looks are priceless. It reminds me of the look I would give my mother when she would note chocolate on my face, and then ask if I had been in the cookie jar.

Owners automatically assume that having their dog on the furniture is a universal wrong. The truth is, having a dog on the furniture can be an enjoyable and relaxing experience. But, it can also foster improper behavior issues, if not done properly. You should allow your dog on the furniture, by invitation only. This will keep him from pouncing on guests or jumping up at the most, inopportune time.

If you want to prohibit your dog on any of your furniture, follow the first step of the following training method. If you want your dog on the furniture, but, only when given permission, follow all of the training method.

To eliminate a dog from being on the furniture you must not allow him access to the furniture when no one is around. This means he must be continually supervised. Jumping on furniture is a self-rewarding behavior and cannot be ignored. The first step is to interrupt the behavior with the least amount of interaction as possible. When your dog jumps on the furniture, gently remove him by slipping your fingers under his collar and guiding him off and onto the floor. Do not give a command nor utter a noise to interrupt this behavior. When he jumps back up, immediately walk over and remove him in this same gentle, but matter of fact, manner. Do not jerk the dog from the furniture; use your whole body to gently move him. The moment he is off the furniture, let go of his collar and walk away. Expect the dog to turn and jump back up onto the furniture, because he is trying to figure out why you are interrupting his behavior. After you have guided him off of the furniture, put him into a time-out. Follow the time-out previously outlined.

Follow through is important. If you begin the process of interruption you must continue until a time-out has been issued and the dog has been released. Do not have different people conducting multiple interruptions within a few minutes of each other. This will teach the dog he does not have to respect your leadership (i.e. when a father steps in to undermine a mother's authority while giving a child consequences). Whoever corrects the dog initially must follow through until the end of the exercise. For example, if your daughter puts a dog in time-out, she must be the one to release the dog from a time out. If you are the person removing the dog from furniture, you must be the one to follow though until the dog chooses to stay off the furniture, or until you release the dog from time-out. When you see your dog choosing to stay on the floor or go to his bed, give him a lot of verbal praise. Praise the behavior you do want when extinguishing one that you do not want. This training may take a week or two. After two weeks, decrease the amount of chances your dog gets before going into a time-out. More stubborn dogs will continue trying, but if you stick with it, they will eventually understand that furniture is off limits. As a matter of definition, being "on the furniture", is three or more feet, not two. If your dog attempts to stand up on the furniture using his two front feet, this is considered a jump, just ignore it because it is not self-rewarding.

To teach your dog to jump onto the furniture by invitation only, choose a specific word for that precise behavior. I use the word "couch" anytime I allow my dog on a piece of furniture. One way to reward a dog for displaying good manners (such as sitting quietly on his bed) is to reward him by allowing him onto the furniture with you. Tap the piece of furniture you want him on and say the command word. It may take your dog a minute to understand what you are asking. When the dog jumps up, praise him.

A few rules do apply once the dog is on the furniture. Do not let him sit on the back of the cushions or along the arms of the couch. He must be respectful and only get into laps of those that invite him. Once he jumps off the furniture, the invitation is no longer valid. When you are ready for furniture time to be over, use another command, such as "off," and gently remove him by the collar.

Soon, your dog will begin to understand the full scope of rules surrounding furniture.

On a side note, I do not recommend allowing the dog on just one piece of furniture without permission. Having a special piece of furniture specifically for the dog is fine, but it should still be by invitation only.

Training in a Multi-Dog Household

Training starts with teaching owners the appropriate way to interact with and set expectations for their dogs. Think of it like any other lifestyle change. It will take time to form new habits, but once established, these skills will help you lay a foundation for any dog in your home. When teaching dogs new rules, train each dog individually before expecting them to do well together. Keep in mind, that even if you do not have problems with all dogs in your household, you should expect the same behavior from each. You should also interact the same way with each so that your habits can form more quickly.

Coming Home

Many owners come home to more than one jumping, barking and dancing dog. Each dog will play off the energy of the other dog, which can cause problems. Humans often get pushed over, backed into a wall or stepped on. This turns the joyous occasion of returning home into a nightmare.

If you leave your dogs out when you are gone they will greet you at the door when they hear you pull in. If your dogs jump or bark when you enter, you should ignore for these inappropriate behaviors. Verbally reward any dog in your home that displays controlled excitement. When acknowledging, stay calm yourself so you do not add to the excitement.

A problem that can occur when arriving home with excitable dogs is indirect aggression.[1] Indirect aggression occurs when one dog is unable to obtain the object of his desire while in a high arousal state. The result of the frustration is typically an attack on the other dog, or sometimes a nearby human. This can cause injury and should not be allowed. To help prevent this problem, isolate one or more dogs on rotation so that each dog is allowed to learn controlled excitement before being expected to do it within the pack.

Remember that regardless of the size of your pack, you should always remain consistent, confident and calm when interacting with or training them. Though they may exhibit moments of inconsistency, you must remain consistent with your habits, and be the leader they need.

---

[1] See page 42 for techniques for dealing with indirect aggression.

One-on-One Time

I often see dogs who have separation anxiety related to being separated from the other dogs in their home. This anxiety often manifests with loss of appetite, lethargy, whimpering, crying or destructive behavior. In order to help prevent this issue, I recommend allowing each dog in your home to have one-on-one time with you. Take dogs on walks or rides separately, or simply take them into the yard or living room to play for a period of time with you. You may leave a Kong stuffed with a treat or another special treat for the dog or dogs left alone. Be sure to reward the dog who has been left alone if he is not displaying signs of separation anxiety during the separation period. Separating your dogs for periods of time will allow each dog to develop confidence and its own personality, and will also allow you to work on real life manners with each dog individually.

Chapter III:

Common Issues in Multi-Dog Homes, and How to Correct Them

Pack Order

Many believe in the dominant pack theory where there is an alpha and an omega. A leadership or pack order is standard within a pack, but is not as black and white as you may think. Though dogs of today descended from wolves, they do not establish a pack order as their ancestors did. This is because we have domesticated them to survive in today's world alongside us. Within a pack there should be leaders and followers. It is rare to have one dog be the overall leader of a pack. Often each dog will choose what is more important to him, and will vie for the leadership spot for that priority. They will, however, give up leadership to another dog for something that is not as important to them. For instance, one dog in your home may be the leader of playtime, while another feels it is important to go out the door first. Keep in mind, that though you are the supreme leader of your household, you should not try to assist between your dogs. For example, just because a dog has been in your home the longest, does not mean he should get everything first (feeding, toys, etc). Likewise, do not show favoritism to a new dog. Allow your dogs to communicate amongst themselves what is important to each. You will only interfere if an inappropriate behavior, such as bullying, occurs.

Bullying

Bullying can happen at any time. It can start when you bring a new dog into your home or your established dog may already be a bully to other dogs he plays with. Bullying occurs when a dog goes overboard to try and establish his leadership skills. Think about great leaders in your life. They do not have to use force or bullying tactics to be good leaders. Bullying among dogs can occur during play, through resource guarding, by excessive mounting and by initiating fights. A dog that bullies is really communicating that he does not have the confidence to maintain control or avoid conflict. He is attempting to show he is "in charge" before conflict has even arisen. Bullies are not necessarily dominant and should not be labeled as such without further evaluation. A dominant dog is one that has natural leadership skills. Keep in mind that not all "bully" breeds are bullies (i.e. bulldogs, pit bulls, etc). This issue can occur with any dog, regardless of size, breed or age.

Here is an example of bullying. Dog A is

playing with Dog B. Dog B is on his back in a wrestling position and is overall in charge of play. Dog A is on top playing nicely. Dog B decides that the play is getting boring so he wants to stop and stand up. When he gives the appropriate signals and begins to get up, Dog A stiffens up, growls, snarls and holds Dog B in position. Dog A is now trying to control the play. He disrespects the signals of Dog B, which is inappropriate.

Bullying is not difficult to resolve and oftentimes does not result in serious issues. It may occur once a day or several times over a month. It is important that you understand what to look for and how to handle it appropriately so it does not become a more serious issue.

When you witness any type of bullying from your dog you must interrupt it immediately. You will always use a calm and confident voice. Begin by using a command such as "that's enough." You will then separate the bully dog from the dog being disrespected. There are a couple of ways you can do this. The first way is by doing a split-up.[2] If you are able to get in-between the two dogs do so and face the bully dog. Without saying anything after your initial "that's enough" command, walk towards the

---

[2] See the DogSpeak YouTube channel (listed in the Resources section of this book) to view a video of this technique.

bully dog until he redirects himself. He may attempt to go around you and towards the other dog. Use your body to calmly interrupt his movement. You will not use your body to block him, so be sure you keep your feet on the floor and do not extend your legs outward. When the bully dog turns and redirects himself you can stop the split-up and also walk away. By doing this you are helping the bully dog learn what you expect when you give the "that's enough" command, as well as what he should be doing when receiving calming signals from another dog. Have a relaxed body and a normal tone of voice. You will do this technique three times in a short amount of time before issuing a time-out. As the days go by, start giving the bully dog fewer chances before a time-out is issued, eventually making the time-out immediate.

When your dog begins to learn that bullying is going to result in consequences you will begin to see him improve. He will begin to exhibit less of the behavior. You should be praising him for choosing to interact appropriately with other dogs. You want him to learn what you would rather see and not just what you do not want to see.

If your dog attends a day care, ensure the staff is trained properly in handling dogs that bully. Ask the manager if the staff understands the signs of bullying and how they handle it.

Rough Play

If you have multiple dogs or if your dog has ever played with another dog, you have more than likely seen rough play. Though loud and rambunctious, it is natural, and typically a non-issue. However, with rough play comes arousal. And when dogs are highly aroused, problems can occur. For instance, if one dog decides he is finished with play, yet a second or third dog is not respecting signals, you must interrupt the dogs who are being disrespectful as they are being bullies. I recommend rough play occur outside as other dogs in the household may become nervous with the commotion, and because the likelihood your grandmother's vase being broken increases.

If you do not want rough play in your home then you must stop the behavior when it occurs. Use the same technique you use to deter bullying. Once you have interrupted the rough play for at least thirty seconds, you can let the dogs outside. Do not interrupt their rough play by letting them outside, otherwise you are rewarding the rough play.

Resource Guarding

This is one of the most common problems I see among multi-dog households. Resource guarding occurs when a dog protects an object from another dog(s) simply because he wants it for himself. Objects can be toys, beds, furniture, chew bones, space or humans. Dogs will exhibit inappropriate behavior when another dog approaches such as growling, snarling, hovering, snapping and biting. Many owners respond to this behavior inappropriately, which increases the chances the behavior will reoccur. When this behavior is allowed to continue, more serious behaviors will follow, including inner-pack aggression.

Look for the following when your dogs interact with one another:

1. Does your dog growl, snarl, snap or bite when another dog approaches him while he's on his bed/couch/human lap?

2. Does your dog growl, snarl, snap or bite when another dog walks past him while he's chewing on a toy/bone/treat?

3. Does your dog protect space such as a doorway or entryway by not allowing other dogs to pass through?

4. Does your dog growl, snarl, snap or bite when another dog tries to play with a toy/another dog or cat?

5. Does your dog not allow others to access a resource such as the water bowl?

Keep in mind, that if Dog A snaps, snarls or growls because Dog B is trying to take something such as toy or bone, and Dog B is either being disrespectful or is ignoring calming signals from Dog A, Dog A may not be resource guarding, but may be reacting to Dog B being a bully.[3]

Here is an example of how to deal with a common type of resource guarding: Dog A is resting nicely on the couch after being given permission to be on the furniture. You then give Dog B permission to be on the couch as well. Before Dog B is able to jump up, Dog A begins growling and snarling at Dog B. Dog A just took possession of something that is not his. You should immediately remove Dog A from the couch by taking him gently by the side of the collar. You do not have to say anything or give the "off" command. The removal is the consequence of his actions. He is not allowed to return to the couch until permission is given. If he displays the same inappropriate behavior three times in a short amount of time, issue a time-out. If you find that you are giving a lot of time-outs for this behavior, take away Dog A's opportunity to get on the furniture for several weeks, and then slowly begin inviting him back. If your dog is sitting in your lap and exhibits this behavior the technique is the same.

---

[3] See the Resources section of this book for more information about calming signals and dog language.

If your dog exhibits this behavior with a dog bed that is on the floor you will immediately remove him from the bed the same way as above. You will implement an immediate timeout, but instead of using a crate you will have him sit with you, on the floor, for a maximum of thirty seconds. Once released from the time-out your dog is welcome to go back to the bed if it is unoccupied, or if he is willing to share with another dog.

If your dog is protecting space and exhibits inappropriate behavior, he will need to be removed from the space the same way you remove him from the dog bed. You will implement a timeout as well. To help curb this behavior, never step over him while he is protecting space, make him move by shuffling your feet underneath him or giving him a "move" command.

If your dog is guarding an object from another dog inappropriately, remove the object from him. Give it back to him when thirty seconds have passed. If the behavior occurs three times in a short amount of time, remove the object for the remainder of the day. Do not give it to the dog that was being bullied, this will only increase the chances of resource guarding taking place again.

I recommend contacting a professional trainer if your dog resource guards you inappropriately.[4]

---

[4] Look for a trainer who uses positive techniques. You can also always email me for recommendations

Indirect Aggression

As mentioned before, indirect aggression occurs when one dog is not getting what he wants and his arousal level is too high. Again, this can result in a dog taking its frustration out on a nearby dog or human. This behavior can occur when you arrive home and one dog cannot reach you, or when your dog is barking and/or jumping at other dogs, human, or other objects outside of a fence, window or door that he cannot reach. In order to prevent indirect aggression, you must be proactive rather than reactive. Use the "that's enough" command and separate using the split up technique. You can also use the collar of the dog. Do not get excited when attempting to interrupt this behavior. Stay calm and confident. Do not attempt to grab your dog by the collar as it is displaying indirect aggression toward another dog, as you may become the target of the indirect aggression.

Interrupting Disagreements

When dogs live together or interact, disagreements and fights will occasionally occur, not unlike in the human world. It is almost impossible to live with multiple dogs without disagreements occurring between the dogs. These disagreements may result in noise and slobber, or

---

for techniques, appointments or research for trainers in your area.

they may result in injury. Disagreements are a normal part of interaction, and you should be prepared to handle them appropriately in order to prevent these disagreements from causing lasting effects to the dogs or harm to others in your home.

Try to remain calm and confident. Do not raise your voice when attempting to interrupt a disagreement. You may use your "that's enough" command, but do so in a calm and confident manner. You may need to raise the volume of your voice so the dogs can hear you, but do not change your tone. If your command does not interrupt the disagreement, you may pull the aggressor away gently by his back legs and gently begin to turn the dog away from the second. Do this *only* if the second dog is not fighting back, and only if you feel confident the aggressor will not display indirect aggression toward you. Do not pull the dog too quickly or roughly so you do not injure one or both dogs involved. If both dogs are participating in the disagreement, use a small air horn to distract the dogs. Give the air horn one quick blast and allow the dogs to separate on their own. Once separated, take the aggressor, or both dogs, to time-out. Do not scream, yell or be aggressive when taking them to their time-out zone. The time-out will last no more than a couple of minutes. If more than two dogs are involved in the disagreement or fight, do not under any circumstances attempt to physically separate the dogs as you may sustain physical harm. Again, use the air horn to distract the dogs. Air horns are typically found in the marina or camping sections of hardware and department stores. If you have questions regarding this technique, please contact me. I cannot stress the importance of keeping yourself and your family safe when disagreements do occur between your dogs.

Many disagreements can be avoided by first teaching a foundation of self-control and by establishing expectations for all dogs in the household.

Inner-pack Aggression

Inner-pack aggression is more serious than an occasional fight, and often causes serious harm to one or both dogs, and anyone who tries to step in. If you have two dogs that fight the instant they are together, and/or have to be constantly separated, you are more than likely dealing with inner-pack aggression. If not properly dealt with, inner-pack aggression can cause a major breakdown within the pack that will result in the rehoming of one or both dogs.

The aggression will begin with fights over space, attention and resources. The fights will be loud, harsh and will often cause injuries. Though the fights may start out as a few times monthly, they will increase to several times a week, to every day to each time the dogs come in contact with one another. Owners will typically begin separating the dogs until the problem is only being managed and not fixed. Managing is not a quick fix and will not work in the long run. There may be times where someone forgets to close a door, lock a gate or put one dog on a leash, and the separation will have been in vain.

Many factors contribute to inner-pack aggression. Many times two dogs are vying for the same positions and neither wants to back down, or a dog has been forced into a position he is not prepared for or wants. Other times, inappropriate behavior has been allowed to continue without proper interruption.

Working on Inner-Pack Aggression

Please be aware that inner-pack aggression cannot always be fixed.[5] At times, rehoming one dog may be the only option you have in order to maintain harmony in your home. However, if you put in time and work, there is a good chance you can redevelop peace among your pack. Again, do

---

[5] I recommend having evaluations done for each dog in your home before you begin any training related to inner-pack aggression. Contact me for more details.

not ever attempt to physically separate two or more dogs who are fighting.

First ensure there is a management plan for the pack. Have a schedule that details when each dog is allowed out with the family and the other is isolated in another area. Be sure the two dogs are not allowed to come in contact with one another, as any conflict can cause injury and/or a step back in any progress that has been made. It is crucial that the entire family follows this plan. Keep in mind, this management strategy is only a temporary fix as you work on changing the dynamics between your dogs.

The next step is ensuring that each human in the house learns to be a confident leader. We are going to establish leadership in a positive way without using fear or the "dominant" theory. There are many ways to establish your leadership during your everyday routine such as feeding, letting outside, going for a walk or letting out of the crate. A true leader is confident, consistent and always follows through. A leader is not fearful or dominating. Your job as the leader is to control and provide all good things for the pack as long as expectations are being met. Whatever your dog sees as a reward, you must control. Teach him to work for the reward before earning it. Greeting people and dogs outside the home may be a big reward for your dog, so this is a great opportunity for you to teach self-control and establish some leadership.

Meeting & Greeting People/Dogs

When meeting or greeting dogs or people, only allow your dog to do so with permission. This will not only help keep you from being pulled down, it will also help with the issue of "chasing," (as in chasing a squirrel or deer), and will assist with self-control.

Self-control that does not impede your ability to communicate with another individual is appropriate behavior. Little to no barking or whining, four-feet-on-the-floor and loose leash manners are a great start. Your permission word can be the same as you use for other exercises. Anytime your dog wants to greet something and it is convenient and appropriate, wait for him to offer a positive, well-mannered behavior. When he does, verbalize the permission word and take him to the object. For instance, you are out for a walk and a see a familiar, friendly dog walking towards you. You note that your dog recognizes his friend and begins to pull towards him. Your dog pulls until they greet, and then you move on with your walk. In this instance, you may not mind that he greets his friend, but you have just allowed him to do so without permission. You are then rewarding inappropriate behavior. A better approach would be the following. You are out for a walk and recognize that same friendly dog. Give your dog permission *before* he has the opportunity to start the inappropriate pulling behavior.

The rules are the same if someone is approaching you and your dog. If it is okay for the human to greet your dog, be sure to give your dog permission before they acknowledge, and subsequently reward any poor behavior. Again, be sure your dog is exhibiting appropriate behavior. If someone approaches your dog and he is not exhibiting good behavior (and hence, has not earned the reward to approach) then create distance from the person and relay that the dog cannot be approached. It is your responsibility to set your dog up for success. To achieve success, you cannot be shy when in public. I find it is much easier to tell people; "sorry, my dog is in training," while taking a step back away from approaching dogs and people. People understand this, and will be appreciative.

When it is not appropriate to greet a passing dog or human, regardless of what your dog is doing, pass by without any hesitation. Create distance when needed to ensure no one rewards your dog for inappropriate behavior or before you are able to give permission.

Once you feel that you have established your leadership it is time to begin working with each dog individually on self-control around other dogs. Working the stationary exercise will teach your dog to make appropriate choices when faced with arousal. You will begin this exercise on-leash anywhere there is distraction and then you will move to a highly distracting area such as the outside area of a dog park.

Stationary Exercise

Use a short leash, a regular or Martingale collar, and a bag of mixed treats. Vary the taste quality of your dog's treats from a value of one to five.

As the leader of this exercise, you are responsible for controlling your immediate environment. Make sure that no one rewards your dog's behavior if it is inappropriate or without permission. You are also responsible for acknowledging the good behavior that your dog is doing. This behavior may be as simple as standing quietly, or sitting nicely while another dog walks by. Look for the incremental parts of a behavior, not just the behavior as a whole. In other words, if you want your dog to sit nicely when another dog approaches, then reward when your dog first looks toward the approaching dog and does not start to lose control. As the dog gets closer, reward your dog for standing quietly. If your dog wags his tail, but does not lunge forward, reward his self-control. Do not wait for the approaching dog to walk by before you reward your dog.

Your goal is to teach your dog how to react to various stimuli he encounters. You ultimately want your dog to learn what behaviors are appropriate without waiting for a command. Independent thinking will transfer to his everyday behavior in the real world. Hopefully, he will choose to forego reacting to stimuli that once had him barking and pulling incessantly. If done correctly, your dog will choose to look to you for a reward. In the real world you want your dog to choose to leave distractions alone without waiting for a command from you.

It is critical that you have an idea as to what behavior you would like to see from your dog during these distracting moments. Before you move further with the exercise, take a moment and think about the behaviors you want to see during the following distractions...

1. As a dog passes.
2. As a human passes.
3. As a human greets your dog.
4. As a dog greets your dog.
5. As a bicycle goes by.
6. As a squirrel (cat, etc) runs by.

You must think realistically when considering the behavior you would and would not like to see from your dog. If you expect your dog to sit every time another dog walks by, then your walks will be inefficient and boring. I recommend that you teach your dog to pass another dog without pulling, barking or lunging. If your dog learns that he cannot greet another dog without permission it will make both your lives much easier.

When working the stationary exercise prepare yourself by dressing appropriately with the appropriate shoes. Wear a soft stable shoe when doing this exercise; a pair that provides comfort and stability. Stand on a flat surface and keep your feet shoulder width apart so that you maintain strength and balance in case your dog pulls at a distraction. Be sure to create enough space between you, your dog and the distractions. Initially, start away from the road where your dog may come in contact with the distractions. The better your dog gets, the closer you can get to the distractions – such as the sidewalk, your neighbor's fence, or a playground.

Refer back to the leash handling skills to ensure you are handling the leash appropriately. Initially, your dog will be overly excited. Stand quietly, and allow your dog to try different behaviors. Some will be inappropriate and will not receive a reward.

Allow your dog time to realize that the behavior he is offering (pulling) is not getting him any closer to the distraction, nor is it getting him the reward treat you have in your pocket. See if he offers a different behavior (barking). If this different behavior is still a behavior you do not want, continue to ignore him. If after a few minutes your dog does not offer an appropriate behavior (standing still for 4 seconds) and continues to offer negative behavior (twisting and jumping), put him in the house in a time-out.

If a positive behavior is exhibited (standing quiet for 4 seconds), acknowledge verbally and then reward with food. Reinforce consistently as long as the dog is offering good behavior. Once the dog is offering an appropriate behavior consistently add seconds in between each verbal acknowledgement, and intermittently disperse the food reward. If at any time your dog offers an inappropriate behavior, cease rewarding and ignore him. Begin the rewarding when he shows repeated good behavior.

If the appropriate behavior is consistent enough to where you are able to count to sixty, between verbal acknowledgements, then you are ready to move toward the distractions. Each movement is only one step forward. Be prepared for your dog to start pulling and lunging when you move forward. This is normal and is expected. Repeat the process; however, this time, if your dog fails to offer the appropriate behavior in the allotted time take a step backwards, instead of going back into the house for a time out. If you do back up, then the reward is verbal praise only and the opportunity to move forward again. Once forward, he earns food rewards, once again.

This exercise can be done for thirty minutes at a time, however; some dogs cannot handle thirty minutes. Do not push your dog too hard. End on a positive note by adjusting the time you work this exercise based on your dog's ability. Too many time-outs may mean you are pushing him too much. You may not make it to the distraction zone the first time, but you are building on the foundation. Keep in mind that each positive step forward is a move towards a dog with ingrained self-control.

This exercise will be difficult for some dogs and may take several weeks to move towards the distraction zone. Once your dog is consistent in one area, such as your front yard, go to somewhere more difficult, such as standing outside the dog park or a playground full of screaming children. The more places you go, the better your dog will become, and the faster he will adjust to unfamiliar distractions.

Re-Introduction

Once each dog has performed well with distractions during the stationary exercises and you feel comfortable in ignoring unwanted behavior and rewarding appropriate behavior, it is time to re-introduce the two dogs that have issues. We will do this slowly and on-leash to ensure proper choices are being made and appropriate behavior is being rewarded.

You will need two adults to work this exercise unless one dog is not the aggressor and would rather avoid the conflict. If you have one dog that is the avoider then you can keep him off-leash and put the aggressor on-leash. For the purpose of the book we will talk about putting both dogs on leash for re-introduction.

Only adults who feel confident should play a part in this process. Each participant will have a short leash, a bag of rewards and focus. Begin the exercise in a room large enough for space between the two dogs. One handler will take one dog and place himself in a seat on one side of the room while the other handler has the other dog and places himself on the opposite side. If the dogs begin to show any type of aggression simply ignore and allow them to choose a different response. If either dog chooses to not change his behavior after a minute remove him from the room. If either dog chooses to change his behavior to something more positive, verbally mark and reward. One dog may show better behavior than the other and should be acknowledged for it. If a dog must be removed only remove for thirty seconds and then reenter giving him another minute to choose a different behavior. If you find that you have to give a time-out to either dog more than three times in a short period then you have either rushed to this step too quickly or the space between the dogs is not large enough. You may have to begin this exercise outside where more space is available.

This exercise is similar to your stationary exercise that you have already practiced. As each dog begins to show better behavior towards each other you will decrease the distance between the two. Each time you move closer be prepared that each dog may choose the inappropriate behavior but he should change to an appropriate one faster each time. You will continue this exercise until you are able to get a few feet between the two dogs without incident. Be sure that you read each dog's body language to ensure that he is relaxed and using his calming signals appropriately. If you are seeing any tightness in your dog's face or your dog looks to be holding his breath, create distance. You want to see your dog relaxed and accepting of the other dog.

Be sure to practice this exercise daily. Each exercise should not be more than ten minutes each. It may take several weeks before you are ready to move to the next step in the reintroduction phase. When both dogs are able to come into the room, on-leash, and immediately sit three feet apart without incident, then you are ready to proceed.

Group Walk

When harmony in the house is better, it is time to begin group walks. This exercise takes two human adults and should never be attempted alone. Each person will have a dog on a short leash and a collar that allows for control. This may be a Gentle Leader head collar or a Martingale collar. Do not use any type of correction collar during this exercise. The dogs will be on the farthest side of you and your partner to allow the two of you to walk side by side. You may need to start with a few feet between you and the other handler. Begin a normal walk together. If the dogs are behaving nicely, verbally praise and reward. If either dog begins to show inappropriate behavior towards the other, stop the walk and work in a stationary position. Create distance until both dogs are behaving appropriately. Once they have calmed you may continue walking with the distance you created. Do this exercise until the dogs are walking several blocks without an incident. Next, take the less aggressive of the two and place him in between the two handlers while the other dog still walks on the farthest side of his handler. When they are comfortable with this you will then place both dogs in the center, with distance so they are unable to reach each other. Remember to verbally praise for appropriate behavior.

Off-Leash Re-Introduction

It is best to do the off-leash re-introduction with a skilled professional. In many cases, it is better that you and other household members are not present. This is because many times your dogs can sense your nervousness. To do this, you may locate a dog daycare that is trained to handle such an introduction. If a daycare is not available, I recommend finding a professional who can assist in an environment such as a small yard or dog park. I do not recommend you attempt this on your own.

When to Seek Professional Advice

One of the main reasons you got another dog was to keep your current dog company and to give him a buddy. However, sometimes dogs just do not connect or have a poor first impression. They may tolerate one another, but they are not particularly smitten. In these cases, do not force the issue. If the two dogs are getting along otherwise, respect their relationship and move forward. They can find other buddies outside of the home through daycare, play dates or the dog park.

Dealing with two dogs that constantly fight, however, is an exhausting battle. It can deplete your energy and can cause a serious lack of confidence. If at any time you find yourself consistently feeling nervous, stressed or unable to implement the techniques I recommend, locate a professional in your area familiar with inner-pack aggression. The professional should use positive methods and should not focus on basic obedience when dealing with the issue. If you are unsure, request references from former clients that have sought his or her advice for this particular issue. Be sure that they do most of their work in the home with you and the dogs, and do not recommend an immediate "boot camp" for the dogs. If you choose a boot camp setting, visit the facility first and observe the way the staff interacts with the dogs. Boot camps should not go for more than a week and follow-up sessions should be done in the home. As always, I am also happy to assist with recommendations.

When to Make the Tough Decision

When dealing with inner-pack aggression there is no guarantee the issue can be resolved completely. If you and a professional feel that the issue is irreversible, you may have no other choice but to rehome one of your dogs. This is not only for the peace and safety of the household but also for the health and happiness of the dogs. You want to ensure that your dogs have the best quality of life possible, and being social is a big part of that. If two dogs living together cannot live harmoniously with the other dogs in the home or with their owners, their quality of life suffers.

I realize this is a very difficult decision, and should not be taken lightly. Keep in mind that just because your dogs do not get along with one another, does not mean they will not get along with dogs in other homes. This is when the individual professional evaluations are extremely useful. Keep in mind, that very few dogs can truly be deemed "vicious," so I do not recommend euthanasia for any dog that is part of inner-pack aggression until this professional evaluation has been done.[6]

---

[6] Again, please contact me for more information and recommendations.

RESOURCES

I hope that this book has brought you much-needed education in order to help smooth life out for your multiple dog household. It can be a real challenge to balance a training schedule but it is imperative that you do so in order to prevent problems from occurring. Below you will find more resources to help educate yourself on dog behavior and training.

E-Mail: Nikki is always more than happy to assist with training questions and/or references: info@dogspeak101.com

Website: For the latest DogSpeak news, visit www.dogspeak101.com

E-Training for Dogs: Bring Nikki's seminars, including "When Love Isn't Enough," and "Understanding Dog Communication" to your home!
www.e-trainingfordogs.com

Facebook: Get the latest news from DogSpeak! www.facebook.com/DogSpeak101

YouTube: Check out exclusive training videos!

www.youtube.com/DogSpeak102

ABOUT THE AUTHOR

Nikki Ivey, professional Dog Trainer/Behavior Consultant is the owner and founder of DogSpeak™. She has been working with dogs and their owners since 1996. She has spread her wealth of knowledge to not only the general public but to the professional pet world as well. She loves to educate individually and in groups, wanting all pet owners and professionals to have a better understanding of dogs and to have the healthiest possible relationship with them.

Nikki has spent many years learning to truly understand the nature of dogs and their motivations. By letting go of the "dominant pack theory" method, she is allowed to be more in tune with dogs, and more effective using her own method of training known as DogSpeak™. Nikki uses positive methods with negative punishment such as time-outs, stopping playtime and taking away attention. She doesn't use any form of physical correction such as correction collars, shock devices or fake bites. This allows dogs to show their true personality, builds their confidence and always leaves them happy. It also ensures that children aren't being taught to be negative or physical with their dogs when teaching.

Nikki believes in clearly communicating with dogs, setting their expectations and giving them a confident leader. She teaches foundation skills to dogs such as self-control and problem solving. Once a solid foundation is in place, you can begin to build the walls of real life manners that go beyond the traditional obedience training of sit, stay, down, come and heel. With real life manners your dog will know how to respond in situations without having to be commanded by you; however, when you do need to command your dog, they respond quickly and enthusiastically.

Nikki also owned and operated the first dog daycare in Tennessee and has spent the last six years helping others build their successful daycares, either from the ground up or as an additive to an existing business. She trains staff members on dog behavior and interaction at daycares, veterinary clinics, and boarding facilities. Local rescue groups and shelters have started taking advantage of the knowledge and skill that Nikki has to help their foster parents understand the importance of foundation skills and being a confident, consistent leader.

In 2001, Nikki founded Tennessee Emergency Rescue and Recovery Association (TERRA), which uses K9s to locate missing persons and deceased individuals in water or land. She's not only a handler of a Human Remains Detection dog but also teaches other handlers to work their dog in HRD.

In addition to teaching, Nikki has also authored articles for various magazines and newspapers, is a handler for KlaasKids, Inc. and the National Center for Missing and Exploited Children.

In her spare time Nikki enjoys writing fiction, and often incorporates her knowledge of search and rescue. Nikki's first novel, *Callout*, is available online at any large bookstore.

The following books are available through Amazon:

When Love Isn't Enough: A guide for dog fosters, rescues and owners

Dealing with Canine Fear and Anxiety

Be Safe, Be Responsible: Understanding Dog Communication

Proper Leash Manners

Adopting a Rescue Dog

Callout

INDEX

Made in the USA
Las Vegas, NV
30 November 2021